Original title:
Finding the Meaning of Life in the Ordinary

Copyright © 2025 Creative Arts Management OÜ
All rights reserved.

Author: Victor Mercer
ISBN HARDBACK: 978-1-80566-286-0
ISBN PAPERBACK: 978-1-80566-581-6

Garden Paths of Discovery

In morning light, the garden wakes,
With dew that sparkles, oh what a sight!
The gnomes stand guard, with silly grins,
As bunnies hop through flowered delights.

A squirrel steals snacks, with cheeky flair,
While ants march like soldiers in a line.
A sunflower bows, as if to declare,
"I'm the best dancer! Just watch me shine!"

The cat sprawls wide on a patch of sun,
Dreaming of mice that darted past.
With a flick of its tail, so cleverly done,
Life's little whispers, they go by fast.

But in the chaos, a laugh is born,
From tiny seeds to fully bloomed fate.
Each tiny moment, a gem to adorn,
Who knew that dirt could hold something great?

Reflections in a Puddle

Staring down at puddles wide,
I see my shoes, my tattered pride.
A world of clouds, upside-down,
Where splashes wear a drippy crown.

Each splash a thought, a laugh, a glee,
Why am I wet? It's all so free!
I dance with ducks, they quack with style,
Life's a giggle, just for a while.

The Art of Everyday Magic

Toast leaps high, butter slides down,
Breakfast magic in my town.
Coffee brews with burps and sighs,
Waking dreams with jittery highs.

The socks in pairs, a rare delight,
Dances with dust bunnies take flight.
Each moment's a trick, life's little jest,
Making the mundane feel like a fest.

In the Embrace of Routine

Alarm clocks hum a morning tune,
Socks lost in the wash, perfect gloom.
My toothbrush whispers, 'We can't stall!'
Rushing to meet the day's loud call.

Lunchboxes bursting, food art displayed,
Leftovers mixing in a parade.
Routine sways in its funky groove,
Each day a dance, a daily move.

Threads of Gold in Daily Life

A cat on a nap, sunbeam lounge,
Watching the world as it spins around.
Cookies crumble, crumbs on my chin,
Messy joys, let this day begin!

The shuffle of feet, a neighbor's cheer,
Mundane tales bring laughter near.
Life's a quilt with patches bright,
In messy threads, we find the light.

Breadcrumbs of Contentment

In the kitchen, crumbs gather round,
Where happiness can sometimes be found.
Leftover pizza and a half-eaten pie,
Who needs a feast when you've got a fry?

The morning coffee spills a little here,
My cat gives me looks, full of cheer.
A burnt toast and a smile so wide,
Life's oddities, I can't help but abide.

The Grace of a Worn-Out Path

Worn-out shoes with stories to share,
Each scuff and scrape, a life laid bare.
Sidewalks whisper secrets unused,
While pigeons tease me, mildly amused.

The postman waves with a jolly grin,
As I stagger home, my journey akin.
With every stumble, I laugh and sway,
Oh, the grace in this clumsy ballet!

The Beauty Beneath Our Feet

A dandelion pops through concrete gray,
   Nature's humor on full display.
With ants in a line, they march with pride,
   While I ponder this odd, lively ride.

A pebble kicks back, "Hey, look at me!"
The mundane turns slightly wild and free.
I trip over roots, still, laughter flows,
   The beauty beneath, everyone knows!

Embracing the Subtle Seasons

The wind howls like a silly fool,
While leaves take a dance, and I join the school.
With scarves slipping off, I embrace the chill,
Life's quirks and quirks, a bundle to spill.

Spring comes, and I sneeze with glee,
As blossoms swirl and flighty bees flee.
I twirl with the flowers, holding my breath,
In each subtle season, there's joy, not death!

Shadows of Yesterday's Dreams

In the shadiest corner I sit,
Missing my youth like an old knitted mitt.
Dreams flee like socks in the dryer,
Yet here I am, a couch-lounging buyer.

With each slice of pizza, I ponder,
How tomorrow could spark more wonder.
Does the cat understand my plight?
Or does she nap through day and night?

Captured Moments in Boring Days

My coffee mug stares with disdain,
As I recount last week's mundane train.
Did I really wear mismatched shoes?
Or is this just what boredom brews?

The toaster pops, a laughter so dry,
As toast rewards the morning sigh.
I dance in the living room—what a sight!
Not even the dog seems to take flight!

Whispers of the Wind Through Trees

The trees gossip as I walk near,
Whispers drift like a laugh in my ear.
Branches wave, 'Look, a squirrel is wise!'
Yet here I am with unshaved thighs.

Leaves swirling down in a comical fray,
Each gust bears witness to my dismay.
"Is that a hidden treasure?" I shout,
Only to find it's just a shoe left out.

A Tapestry of Simple Acts

Each chore I do feels like a feat,
Turning laundry day into a rhythmic beat.
The vacuum sings a humorous tune,
As I pretend to tango with the broom.

In these moments, laughter spills wide,
Life's little wins we can't always hide.
I wave to my neighbor, who's gardening bold,
Giggling at weeds that refuse to be told.

Conversations with the Unseen

I spoke to a spoon, it looked quite sweet,
'Tell me your secrets, are they a treat?'
It jingled with laughter, said, 'Just stir the soup,
And life will surprise you, join in the loop.'

A sock asked a shoe, 'What's your grand plan?'
He chuckled and said, 'To dance if I can!'
Together they shuffled, a waltz on the floor,
To the rhythm of dust bunnies, who begged for more.

Mosaic of Ordinary Wonders

A pebble rolled over, smirked at my shoe,
'What's a day without me? Just ask the dew!'
It twinkled and winked, a gem in disguise,
Promising treasures and surprises that rise.

A leaf in the breeze whispered secrets so light,
'Watch me twirl, oh, what a glorious flight!'
It danced on the air, a mossy ballet,
Making mundane moments feel like a parade.

In Praise of the Gentle Hour

At dusk the cat pondered, her thoughts quite profound,
'Life's just a nap on this soft, cozy ground.'
While dreaming of fish, she forgot her great plight,
To pounce on the world, a comical sight.

Tea cups confided, 'We brew happiness here,
Our warm little whispers chase away any fear.'
With biscuits for buddies, they chuckled and scoffed,
Simple joys abound, and laughter was soft.

A Symphony of Simple Sounds

The kettle sang softly, a tune so divine,
'Life's bubbling magic, oh, don't you feel fine?'
A tick-tock from clocks, in a chorus of cheer,
Reminding us all that the fun starts right here.

The fridge hummed a ballad, cool rhythms in place,
'Just grab a sweet snack, it's a treat to embrace!'
And the microwave beeped, in a dance of delight,
Making meals out of moments, oh what a sight!

The Magic in Morning Rituals

Each sunrise brings a brand new cup,
While toast pops up and pets stir up.
I dance with jams and spread the butter,
The kitchen sings, oh what a clutter!

Brewed coffee that might just be magic,
Every sip feels rather tragic.
Why does the milk always froth so high?
It's a cappuccino made to fly!

As I search for socks that match,
This daily quest feels quite the catch.
The dog looks on, amused and wise,
In this chaos, joy surely lies.

So cheers to mornings, messy and bright,
With creaky floors and sleepy light.
Who knew the day could start so grand?
In simple ways, bliss is close at hand.

Reflections in a Coffee Cup

I stare into my coffee's pool,
Its dark depths play the endless fool.
I ponder life and all its perks,
While debating if I'll skip my works.

A swirl of cream creates a show,
Like swirling thoughts, they ebb and flow.
With each sip, a chuckle comes,
Did I just hear my coffee hum?

Caffeine dreams and sugar highs,
Lost in the thoughts of 'What is wise?'
Instead of answers, I just grin,
'Cause life's a race, but where to begin?

The bottom's filled with grounds and sighs,
Yet in the muck, true laughter lies.
Here's to the brews, both bold and strong,
In every cup, we all belong.

The Sway of a Garden Breeze

In the garden, the daisies dance,
They flirt with bees, so keen to prance.
The wind's a jester, to and fro,
Tickling petals, come on, let's go!

A squirrel steals seeds, with utmost glee,
While I wonder, what's wrong with me?
It's a comedy of plants and pests,
Life seems best in garden quests.

A ladybug, my tiny friend,
Lands on my shoulder, no need to pretend.
With every laugh from nature's crew,
I learn that joy is found in view.

So here's to breezes, sunny and light,
Tickling laughter into our sight.
In every sway, an embrace we find,
A perfect moment, body and mind.

Stories Hidden in Side Streets

On side streets where the shadows play,
You'd find a cat that rules the day.
With every step I take to see,
The absurdity of sheer glee.

The pavement cracks with tales untold,
A lost shoe sparkles, bright and bold.
While children giggle, racing near,
These moments sparkle, full of cheer.

Old lampposts lean with souvenirs,
Of laughter, tears, and best of years.
I trip on dreams that flit and glide,
In the mundane, magic can't hide.

I wander on, my heart a map,
Through silly signs and quirky chap.
In every nook, the world weaves tight,
A tapestry of sheer delight.

Echoes of Soft Laughter

In the kitchen, pots do sing,
A dance of spoons, oh what a fling!
Spaghetti tango on the stove,
Who knew such chaos could improve?

The dog, he prances like a fool,
Chasing shadows, yes, he's the tool!
Lost his tail in a game of chase,
Oh, the wonders of this silly space!

Friends come over, tea in hand,
We laugh at life, we take a stand.
Burnt the toast, we cheer with glee,
Toast or not, it's good company!

In moments small, we find the bright,
Laughter echoes through the night.
Who needs a grand and fancy show?
In soft laughter, joy will grow!

Sunlight Through the Windowpane

Morning rays peek through the blinds,
Tickling dust in joyful finds.
Coffee brews, a fragrant spell,
Life's a circus; oh, can't you tell?

Jelly spills upon the floor,
A sticky mess we can't ignore.
Cat dances on the kitchen ledge,
Just don't fall, we all allege!

Mom's old jokes that never fade,
Are like sweet candy, homemade.
We roll our eyes but laugh out loud,
In this madness, we feel proud!

Sunlight streams, the day is bright,
Finding joy in silly sights.
With every giggle, life takes flight,
In these moments, everything's right!

Ordinary Moments, Extraordinary Light

A sock that disappears from view,
Is quite the talent, who knew?
Chasing it beneath the bed,
Comedic treasure, joy instead!

The fridge hums a soothing tune,
As leftovers dance under the moon.
Each bite a journey, flavors collide,
In every meal, magic can hide!

Rainy days with puddles wide,
Splish-splash boots, we take a ride.
Jumping high, we make a splash,
In these moments, we feel the cash!

Life's simple acts, they spark delight,
In every shadow, there's a light.
Through giggles shared and laughter bright,
We find the joy that feels just right!

The Heartbeat of Common Days

Alarm bells ringing, rise and shine!
Sleepy heads in denial align.
Drop the toast, a crumbly plight,
Oh, breakfast fun – what a sight!

Neighbors argue over the fence,
Mysteries gleefully intense.
We laugh at gossip overheard,
Life's a tale that's often absurd!

Old shoes chasing the morning sun,
Worn-out soles but oh, what fun!
Every step a silly dance,
In the mundane, we find romance!

So here's to days both dull and bright,
In each heartbeat, we find delight.
With laughter shared, come what may,
Joy lives loud in common days!

Revelations in Routine

Waking up to daily fuss,
Coffee spills, oh what a plus!
Socks that clash, a sight to see,
In chaos, hints of glee.

Toothpaste blobs in morning light,
Brushing teeth, a comic sight.
Chasing kids, they flee with speed,
Life's a circus, and we lead.

Dinner plans that go awry,
Burnt toast leaks a smoky sigh.
Laughter bubbles through the mess,
In the wreckage, we confess.

Even chores bring silly joy,
Folding laundry like a ploy.
In mundane acts, we see the clue,
The magic lies in all we do.

Treasures Beneath the Surface

In the pantry, snacks find their way,
Hidden gems for a dreary day.
A half-eaten sandwich, stale and bold,
Turns into a feast worth gold!

Dust bunnies dance under the bed,
A treasure map, where laughter's spread.
Old toys whisper tales of fun,
Gone are worries, here comes the sun!

Mismatched spoons in a kitchen drawer,
Each one tells a story, and more.
A pot that boils over, a splashy scene,
In these messy moments, life's routine.

Underneath the mundane clutter,
A quirky spark, just like butter!
Life's simple joys, we learn to embrace,
In each quirky twist, we find our place.

Light Through Kitchen Windows

Morning rays through greasy panes,
Chasing shadows, playing games.
Scrubbing pots with all my might,
Enlightenment from a greasy sight!

Birds chirp loud while I prepare,
Breakfast chaos fills the air.
Eggs that splatter, toast that burns,
In this mess, how laughter churns!

Chucking crumbs to eager pets,
They leap and bound, no regrets.
Pans that clang like kitchen bells,
In discord, joy and laughter dwells.

Sunbeams flirt with floury hands,
Mixing hope with kitchen plans.
In this frolic of daily grind,
The sweetest moments we can find.

The Poetry of Serving Tea

Boiling water, a bubbling song,
Teacups stacked, where they belong.
A splash of milk, a spoonful sweet,
In every sip, life's tales repeat.

Pouring spice with hands that shake,
An accidental splash—oh what a quake!
Laughter spills from every side,
In these moments, hearts collide.

Sipping slowly, tales unwind,
In tepid cups, our truths we find.
Friends gather close, with stories to share,
In every sip, we breathe the air.

Seasons change with every blend,
A cup of cheer, a friend to mend.
In the ritual, joy's been sewn,
In tea's embrace, we're never alone.

Stillness in the Silence

In the morning light, tea spills,
A cat sprawls wide, ignoring my drills.
Spatulas dance on the kitchen wall,
I hope the neighbors don't hear my call.

The toaster pops, a slice of fate,
Jam's a-rolling, yet it's still late.
A perfect plan, a brave new world,
But there's a sock, odd and twirled.

The clock ticks loud, as if to tease,
It knows my dreams as much as my knees.
I ponder great thoughts, like 'why is he here?'
Life is odd, yet brings me cheer.

Outside, the squirrels plot their heist,
Gathering crumbs, oh, aren't they nice?
In stillness I sit, in laughter I dwell,
Finding joy in the tales they tell.

Fleeting Glimpses of Joy

A raindrop splashes, a world anew,
Splashing in puddles, oh, how we grew.
Chasing the sun that hides with glee,
A war between clouds and cats, you see?

A sandwich flies through the air, oh dear,
Mustard protests, while bread shows fear.
Each bite's a gamble, a treasure to find,
Or maybe it's just lunch, unrefined.

In the bustle of work, a paperclip spins,
A paper airplane starts as my grin begins.
A dog barks loudly, convinced he's profound,
Yet all I hear is a hilarious sound.

Between quiet moments, laughter breaks through,
Life's little antics, a quirky view.
With each little jest, we dance and sway,
The funny is magic, come what may.

Beneath the Surface of the Mundane

Laundry baskets grow like mountains high,
Fuzzy socks hide as I let out a sigh.
The vacuum roars, a beast in my lair,
Yet dust bunnies laugh, floating in air.

My to-do list is a monster's feast,
Eating my time, a gluttonous beast.
I scribble a joke in between each chore,
Life's sense of humor? It's not a bore.

A chair squeaks loud, it tells its own tale,
Of tight spandex pants and that time I failed.
I giggle at memories, bright as the sun,
In this quirky world, there's always fun.

And when the day ends, I sit and reflect,
On the silliness that we often neglect.
In the ordinary chaos, warmth does reside,
As laughter and joy become our guide.

Tapestries of Lived Experience

Grandma's knitting, a loop and a purl,
Each stitch whispers stories, anchors the whirl.
The yarn entwines like life's little quirks,
With laughter and comfort, it silently lurks.

A spilled drink becomes a masterpiece,
With coffee stains, our worries decrease.
Each drop expands to a giggly scene,
A canvas of life, splattered and keen.

Neighbors bicker, a soap opera airs,
Over parking spots, and backyard chairs.
But amidst the chaos, a chorus of sighs,
Laughter erupts as each moment flies.

As shadows grow long, and day bids adieu,
I ponder the joy in every hullabaloo.
In the whims of existence, laughter's embrace,
We weave our stories, a colorful race.

Small Wonders Unveiled

A sock on the floor, its partner unknown,
It dances alone, in a world of its own.
The cat plays with dust, a grand ballet,
In the corners of chaos, he steals the day.

The jam jar's a treasure, with secrets inside,
A spoonful of laughter, let's take it for a ride.
Each crumb on the counter, a story to tell,
In crumbs we discover, a life lived so well.

The chirp of a bird, as it argues with air,
A whisper of nonsense, who really can care?
The leaves swirl around like they're lost on a trip,
In the journey of silliness, let's take a dip.

So let's pause a moment, life's quirks in our sight,
In marshmallow clouds, and in dog barks at night.
For joy is in chaos, and giggles delight,
In small wonders unveiled, life feels just right.

A Symphony of the Simple

A spoon in the soup, it's a dance on the rim,
The carrots all hum, sometimes they feel grim.
A fork does a jig, on a plate full of cheer,
While the napkin's gossiping, 'Did you hear?'

The clock ticks a joke; it's running late,
Each minute a giggle, a comical fate.
The fridge hums a tune, its door swings wide,
Oh, the melodies hidden where leftovers abide.

The lightbulb flickers, with a wink and a grin,
A shadow goes shopping, what trouble to begin!
The couch cushions giggle, they puff out a sigh,
In a symphony of simple, we laugh till we cry.

So throw on your socks, one blue and one red,
Dance through the moments, let whimsy be spread.
In every small misstep, a song we'll compile,
A symphony of the simple, oh life has its style.

Life's Unwritten Verses

The sneakers are chatting, on the porch they do rest,
One thinks he's a poet, the other the best.
The doorbell rings laughter, with each cheerful chime,
As we pen down the moments, in rhythm and rhyme.

A sneeze like a trumpet, a cough like a flute,
In the orchestra of life, we play with our suit.
The dog thinks he's Shakespeare, with every loud bark,
While the cat, quite the critic, observes from the dark.

The toast pops up singing a crispy refrain,
With butter as the soloist, spreading joy on the grain.
The blender hums softly, composing a sweet song,
In the kitchen, our stage, where we all just belong.

So gather the verses, let the laughter unfold,
In the oddities here, pure magic behold.
For life's unwritten verses, they're never rehearsed,
A comic performance, where joy's always burst.

Ordinary Threads of Infinity

A mug on the table, cracked but a friend,
It cradles the coffee, the day's perfect blend.
A sock on the wall, now a painting so bold,
In threads of the mundane, strange stories unfold.

The calendar lies, with its dates all a mess,
It claims it's Monday, but really, who's stressed?
The fridge holds ambitions, of leftovers past,
In each tiny corner, the moments are vast.

The doorknob spins jokes, as it's opened with grace,
Calling the cat, 'You're late for your race!'
A sprinkle of chaos, a dash of delight,
In ordinary threads, the heart takes flight.

So let's tumble through life, with a wink and a grin,
In each simple action, let the joy begin.
For in every dull moment, infinity lies,
In the humor of living, let laughter arise.

Whispers in the Everyday

A sock's rebellion on the floor,
Takes me laughing out the door.
The cat's knickknacks, a grand display,
Stolen moments, joy at play.

The neighbor's dog with eyes so wise,
Calculates in barks and sighs.
An ant parade on the sidewalk hot,
Each tiny march reveals a dot.

A coffee cup with lipstick stains,
Holds the secrets of mundane gains.
A sandwich dance, a mustard twirl,
In this chaos, life can unfurl.

So raise a glass to the daily grind,
In the giggles, the laughs we find.
For joy's in crumbs and coffee spills,
And every task that time distills.

Chasing Shadows of Simplicity

In a cereal bowl, treasures lie,
Frosted shapes that wink and sigh.
The spoon's a ship on milky seas,
As I sail the morning breeze.

A dust bunny winks from below,
Pretending it's a fluffy show.
Lost socks tumble, a pair in flight,
Chasing dreams into the night.

The neighbor's hen clucks, a mad ballet,
As she trains for the grand parade.
I can't resist a wobbly jig,
Life's little jest, a joyous gig.

So here I sit, pen in hand,
Sketching antics that life has planned.
In every laugh, a simple bliss,
In ordinary tales, nothing goes amiss.

The Poetry of Morning Coffee

Steam swirls like a whispering dream,
In my cup, life's gentle theme.
The first sip, a warm embrace,
Woke up late, but still got grace.

A toast to the crumbs on my shirt,
Like badges earned from morning's flirt.
The dog sniffs out my coffee fate,
With hopeful eyes, he hesitates.

Each drip echoes thoughts profound,
In the ordinary, joy's unbound.
A spoon does a jig, the sugar's sweet,
In chaos found, my heart's a beat.

As laughter spills like cream on brew,
I find delight in each new view.
So here's to life's quirky blend,
In every cup, a cherished friend.

Unraveled Threads of Routine

Alarm bells scream, a morning fight,
The bed's a cloud, so warm and bright.
I wrestle with sheets, a nightly foe,
With pajama legs tangled in tow.

A mismatch of shoes, a quirky pair,
Dance to the door, without a care.
In the simplest things, joy plays peek,
Like socks in the dryer, a game unique.

Chasing the sun, I trip on a toy,
A tumble and laugh, oh what a joy.
The mailman grins, a nod and wave,
In the quirks, it's love we save.

So as days roll, let laughter lead,
In each glance, let adventure breed.
For in every scramble, a truth we see,
Life's a comedy, wild and free.

Unveiling Hidden Joys

In the morning light, a toast so crisp,
Butter makes each bite a joyful wisp.
A sock lost in the dryer, what a show,
It's a dance of fabric as it swirls below.

Cats play ninja, with each gentle pounce,
Knocking over plants just to see them bounce.
We find the laughter in the simplest things,
As a spoon breaks its silence, and the coffee sings.

Watching ants march with purpose so grand,
They carry picnic crumbs, an organized band.
In every moment, there's a smile to invest,
Even if it's just laughing at a shoe on your chest.

There's joy in the jumbled mess of a room,
Where puzzles lie scattered, a colorful bloom.
A t-shirt that's stained tells a story or two,
Of spaghetti nights and the sauce on your shoe.

Finding Gold in the Grit

Life's little traps are where treasures reside,
Like the crumbs on your shirt that you try to hide.
A coffee cup's crack is a badge of great cheer,
It's a reminder you've caffeinated with fear.

Dust bunnies gather like the best of friends,
They whisper sweet secrets as the daylight bends.
The dog chases shadows, a ridiculous sight,
As you burst out laughing, forgetting your plight.

Old shoes by the door, they've traveled so far,
Each scuff a reminder, each scratch a strange star.
In the chaos of life, there's beauty, it's true,
Like the art on the fridge—a masterpiece stew.

Every smile is gold in the grit of the day,
Like a raindrop that sparkles while dancing on clay.
The world's little quirks bring a glimmer so bright,
In mundane mishaps, we find sheer delight.

Embracing Silence and Solitude

In a quiet room, the clock does its tease,
Each tick a reminder of time's subtle breeze.
The toaster pops bread with a jubilant cheer,
While the fridge hums a tune you never hear.

A favorite chair sighs with a grumpy old creak,
As you ponder the meaning through broken antique.
The lonely sock waits, it's a patient little mate,
Dreaming of its twin, but that's just fate.

In solitude's grip, you'll find laughter's tune,
As the dust gathers stories of a soft afternoon.
A teacup held dearly, your silent best friend,
In stillness, you'll find the joy that won't end.

Even when silence seems heavy like lead,
The whispers of laughter can dance in your head.
For within the quiet, a symphony plays,
In the simplest of moments, you'll find playful ways.

The Color of Still Waters

The pond reflects clouds, a watercolor blend,
Where frogs drop their thoughts, and the ripples extend.
A leaf takes a dive, it's a grand Olympic show,
Who knew that the pond had a talent to bestow?

Fishing for dreams with a stick and some string,
You catch nothing but thoughts, oh, what joy they bring!
The dragonflies dance, in a reality twist,
In shades of bright colors, they flutter and flit.

The sunbeams poke holes in the water's thick veil,
While the turtles just laugh, as they tell their own tale.
A moment of peace, splashed with hues all around,
Embracing this stillness, true magic is found.

With giggles abound and a splash of pure glee,
The water reflects all that you dream it can be.
In the ordinary moments, joy often flows,
And the spirit of playfulness endlessly grows.

Little Gardens of Gratitude

In the soil of simple days,
We plant our seeds with clumsy ways.
A dandelion's crown, proud and grand,
Becomes a throne in a child's hand.

The cat looks stern, a wise old sage,
With paw raised high, it takes the stage.
While sock puppets giggle and prance,
They hold court in a fanciful dance.

A spilled drink, a laugh, a mess,
Life's little quirks, we must confess.
Like kitchen chaos, we create,
A recipe for joy on a plate.

Through tangled yarns and yellowed pages,
We find the laugh in all our stages.
In little gardens, we sow delight,
Forget the sorrow, embrace the light.

Whispers of the Unnoticed

A speck of dust, a gentle breeze,
Whispers secrets from the trees.
The squeaky chair knows all my dreams,
And giggles softly, or so it seems.

Coffee spills, and oh what fun!
A polka dot on my shirt, I'm done.
The morning toast, burnt on one side,
Becomes a smile I can't hide.

The wandering socks hold hands at night,
In a cozy corner, out of sight.
Napping cats, soft piles of fur,
Who knew a purr could cause a stir?

Lost keys dance, they love the chase,
A scavenger hunt in our own space.
In these whispers, we find our glee,
The unnoticed, our comedy.

Echoes of Fleeting Moments

A hiccup at lunch seems out of place,
Turns into giggles, a silly race.
The clock ticks loud, a mocking tune,
As we juggle tasks 'neath a bright afternoon.

Birds on wires, they crack a joke,
One drops a twig, the other spoke.
Laughter echoes, sweet and clear,
In moments fleeting, we hold dear.

Toasts that tumble, wine makes a splash,
Fridge raids at midnight lead to a crash.
Each bite savored, experience gleaned,
In echoes of laughter, joy intervened.

A dance with the mop, a banter with bread,
Who knew that life could be so well-fed?
In every mishap, a treasure we weave,
In fleeting moments, we learn to believe.

Beauty in the Brushstrokes of Life

A splash of paint on a tired wall,
Turns drab to fab, oh what a ball!
With crayons scribbled, we dance around,
Artistry blooms from the lost and found.

A friendly mug, chipped but so bright,
Holds stories of mornings wrapped in light.
While cookie crumbs fall, sprinkles fly,
The messiest baking makes the best pie.

Fluffy pancakes stacked to the sky,
Each syrup drip sings a sweet lullaby.
A dance with the whisk, and flour in air,
Turns breakfast into a whimsical affair.

In clumsy strokes, we paint our days,
With laughter and joy in a million ways.
The beauty lies in mishaps, no doubt,
In brushstrokes of life, we scream and shout.

Savoring the Flavor of Small Things

A crumb on my plate, a chocolate chip,
Sipping cocoa, letting the worries slip.
Mismatched socks and jumbled keys,
I giggle at life, with all its quirks and krill.

The cat in the sun, chasing a fly,
A paper hat that looks like a pie.
Forks that dance on spaghetti strands,
Life's silliness fills up our hands.

A bird on a wire, strumming a tune,
Wiggly worms just relaxing at noon.
Unexpected laughs in a mundane chat,
Embrace all the moments, quirky and fat.

So here's to the crumbs and the misplaced shoes,
To laughter that bubbles and silly snooze.
A wink to the silly, a nod to absurd,
In small things we stumble, life's sweet unheard.

Dances of Dust in Sunbeams

Dust bunnies roll, on floorboards they prance,
A waltz in the light, a dust-induced dance.
Grandma's old slippers, a sight to behold,
As they shuffle along, stories unfold.

The toaster pops up, a breakfast delight,
With toast on its head, it's quite the sight.
Socks in the dryer, a rumble and toss,
Two pairs waltz out; one always gets lost.

The dog with a stick, oh what a scene,
He gallops with joy, a canine routine.
In bubbles of laughter, we find our way,
Dust in the air filters life's grey away.

So let's take a moment, to twirl with the dirt,
In sunbeams we sway, without an alert.
These dances of dust, with giggles unfurled,
Bring magic and joy to an ordinary world.

The Little Things That Spark

A butterfly lands, on a cracked old chair,
Wings painted brightly, with time to spare.
Laughter spills out, from a child's puzzled face,
As they ponder life's mysteries in a reckless race.

An ice cream cone, drips down my hand,
Sticky and sweet, life's small reprimand.
The sound of a sneeze, from a grandpa's old chair,
A burst of delight, fills the summer air.

A penny found glimmers, in cracks of the street,
Collecting small treasures, life feels so sweet.
The evening sun sets, painting the sky,
With laughter like fireflies, darting nearby.

So raise a toast to the sparks of the day,
A wink from a stranger, or laughter's ballet.
In little things, magic and love we embark,
For life's simple joys ignite every spark.

Ashes of Yesterday

Leftover pizza, a cold little treat,
The laughter of friends makes the evening complete.
A burnt loaf of bread, it crumbles in stacks,
As we reminisce over yesterday's hacks.

Old socks in the drawer, a faded romance,
They once danced with feet, now lost in the trance.
Pictures of moments in crooked frames smile,
Reminding us life's worth each silly mile.

A coffee stain here, a ding on the wall,
Add stories to places, both big and small.
The cat's tragic leap, from the couch to the floor,
Leaves us in stitches, with giggles galore.

So here's to the past, with ashes we toss,
To memories made in laughter's sweet gloss.
With a wink to tomorrow, let baggage grow light,
In the mess of our days, life blooms ever bright.

Hopes of Tomorrow

A sprout in the garden, pokes through the dirt,
With dreams of a flower, though started in hurt.
The little seed giggles, at worms in a dance,
While hoping for sunshine, it takes its chance.

My coffee's too cold, but the cat doesn't care,
He snoozes away without any flair.
Dishes pile up like mountains of pride,
As we plan the next trip we dream to slide.

A squirrel does yoga, on a branch full of glee,
Flexing in sunlight, so wild and free.
With waiting and wishing, and snacks on the side,
Tomorrow's a mystery, a fun joyride.

So let's toast to the hopes that wiggle and sway,
To biscuits in tea, and the joy of the day.
In life's little moments find laughter, don't borrow,
For in each small adventure lies hope for tomorrow.

Distant Lighthouses of the Heart

In a coffee cup, a world awaits,
Dreams float like foam on the plates.
A spoon does a jig, as I sip with glee,
Wishing my chores danced like me.

The laundry sings a ballad of blues,
While dust bunnies form their own little crews.
My vacuum's a monster, but I laugh with glee,
As it gobbles up crumbs that once laughed at me.

A cat sprawls lazily in a sunbeam's embrace,
Claiming the couch as its own special place.
With every stretch, it seems to declare,
Life's a soft pillow without a care.

And so I find joy in each silly mess,
In the dance of the mundane, I feel truly blessed.
The lighthouses flicker, guiding my heart,
In the laughter that echoes, I play my part.

Paintbrushes of Everyday Joy

A spatula flips with a flourish so grand,
Creating a feast with the wave of a hand.
Onions may cry, but I'm laughing out loud,
Cooking's my canvas, and I'm feeling proud.

The toaster pops up a slice with flair,
Like a magician pulling a rabbit from air.
Butter slides down in a yellow cascade,
Each breakfast a masterpiece, joyfully made.

Puddles reflect skies painted gray,
But I jump right in and splash all the way.
With each little giggle, under clouds I run,
Finding color in drizzle, oh what fun!

And when the day ends with socks slightly askew,
I'll dance through the chaos, just me and my shoe.
Laughing at life, with its quirks on display,
In the paint of the ordinary, I find my way.

Ordinary Souls in Extraordinary Light

Grocery carts roll like chariots bold,
Foraging treasures in the aisles of gold.
Each item a story, from bread to tart,
Riding the waves of a cart-pushing art.

Old dogs chase squirrels that mock their slow pace,
While kids spin like tops, full of joy's grace.
A sweet elderly couple shares ice cream delight,
In a world spinning fast, they shine so bright.

Bikes wobble past with a giggle and cheer,
Laughter's the music that everyone hears.
From sidewalk to streetlights, joy takes its flight,
In ordinary souls glowing under the light.

And when the sun dips, painting skies with flair,
We gather our stories, savoring air.
For in the simple moments, hearts take their flight,
Transforming the mundane into sheer delight.

Embracing the Ebb and Flow

The dishwasher hums a lullaby sweet,
Plates pirouette in a bubbly retreat.
The mop does a tango on the kitchen floor,
Each swipe a reminder of life's playful score.

Rain taps a rhythm on my windowpane,
In puddles, reflections dance without shame.
I splash with abandon, a child in disguise,
Letting the laughter rain down from the skies.

The neighbor's dog barks in a fit of delight,
Conspiring with squirrels in their acorn-filled flight.
With every bark, the world seems to cheer,
In the chaos of life, there's nothing to fear.

So here's to the moments, both silly and bright,
To falling and laughing, to gaining our sight.
For in the tide's magic, we learn to bestow,
Joy in the journey, embracing the flow.

Color in the Gray

In the morning rush with mismatched socks,
I sip my coffee and dodge the clocks.
A splash of jam on toast that's burnt,
Tastes better than dreams that never learn.

Pigeons strut like they own the street,
While I trip over my own two feet.
The sun peeks through a cloudy veil,
And laughter echoes like a windblown sail.

Bodhi in the Banal

Washing dishes, I find my muse,
An epic tale in leftover stews.
Each soapy bubble a bright delight,
As I dance with spoons in twilight's light.

The dryer hums a gentle tune,
While I ponder why we call it noon.
A sock escapes, a rebel at heart,
In the mundane, I've mastered the art.

Everyday Epiphanies

The cat has claimed my warmest chair,
While I freeze, unaware of despair.
She naps like royalty, dreams that soar,
While I chase crumbs from the floor.

A spider spins in the corner tight,
Creating webs, a wondrous sight.
I wonder if she dreams of flies,
Or just concocts her clever lies.

The Taste of Simple Pleasures

A slice of pizza with extra cheese,
Is like a hug from the softest breeze.
I savor bites, with eyes shut tight,
Every bite feels like pure delight.

In the park, kids chase their dreams,
While ice cream drips with crispy seams.
Laughter bubbles, as birds take flight,
In these moments, all feels just right.

The Radiance of Small Acts

A smile from the barista, bright as the sun,
Coffee spills laughter, the day's just begun.
A cat on the windowsill, napping with glee,
Chasing dust motes, oh, what a sight to see!

The old man on the corner, sharing a tale,
With pigeons as listeners, they never fail.
Sidewalk chalk drawings, a dog's sky-high leap,
Moments so simple, they're treasures to keep.

The echoes of laughter in a crowded café,
Glances exchanged that brighten the gray.
A kid in a splash park, leaping with flair,
Life's ridiculous humor is hiding right there!

So gather the giggles and cherish the cheer,
In moments forgotten, find joy that is near.
For each little blink of this wild, merry ride,
Holds meaning that sparkles, just waiting inside.

Finding Light in the Shadows.

Rainy days clatter, umbrellas in flight,
Puddles become oceans, oh what a sight!
A squirrel on a quest for a nut with a grin,
Dances round raindrops, let the fun begin!

The postman, a hero in his bright yellow coat,
Brings letters of nonsense, oh what do they tote?
Each mail is a mystery, wrapped up tight,
Even bills wear a laugh, in the soft morning light!

Mom's complaints swirl like spaghetti on a fork,
She juggles the laundry while keeping the snark!
A dance in the kitchen, the dog's joyful bark,
Life's silly rhythms make our smiles spark.

Through chinks in the armor of everyday fuss,
The brilliance of banter in chaos makes us.
So when gloom tries to settle, let mischief take charge,
For joy's just a quirk, and it's always at large!

Whispers in the Everyday

A knock at the door, the neighbors all chat,
Baking a cake, with a measured mishap.
Flour on noses, the laughter erupts,
Life's little boons in the mayhem just bust!

Traffic jams happen, but here's a surprise,
Dancing in cars, oh those impromptu highs!
Some belt out their favorites, the horn adds a twist,
Oh, what a chorus, can't let it be missed!

The kid with his crayons, a masterpiece spread,
Coloring life with each stroke, joy ahead!
A whiff of the roses on a walk through the park,
Squirrels put on shows, it's all quite the lark!

So laugh at the simple, the quirky, the plain,
For in every odd moment, there's wisdom to gain.
With giggles and winks as the world spins around,
In the rhythm of ruckus, our truths can be found.

Secrets of the Mundane

The toast pops up, like a magic surprise,
Butter's a wizard, melting before our eyes.
A cat's sleepy yawn, the world's softest sound,
In mornings like these, pure joy can be found.

The sock monster strikes, my drawer is a mess,
Half of the pairs now dwell in distress.
Yet who really needs them when fun's in the chase,
The hunt for a match is a treasure of grace!

Dishes piled high, resembling a tower,
Yet find me a joke in this sudsy shower.
With suds that turn battles into bubble fights,
Each scrub becomes laughter, perfumed in delights.

So here's to the secrets in all we dismiss,
To the giggles hidden in the mundane bliss.
For life, oh so silly, is waiting to play,
In each daily dopiness, joy finds its way!

The Heartbeat of Everyday Life

In the rustle of the morning toast,
Eager crumbs debate, who is the host?
Coffee brews with a funny frown,
While socks revolt and tumble down.

A dance of dust bunnies in the light,
Chasing one another, what a sight!
The clock's tick mocks with zestful chime,
As I struggle to fold this laundry in time.

They say each moment holds a tale,
Even if it's a cat who's gone pale.
In every hiccup, a chuckle hides,
With hiccups and giggles, the day abides.

So let's embrace the silly spree,
Juggling the mundane with glee!
Life's rich peppered with giggling jigs,
In the heartbeat of ordinary digs.

Sunlight on Sidewalks

Sunlight spills like butter on the street,
Where ants form parades with tiny feet.
A mailbox grins, sporting a hat,
As birds critique my slow morning pat.

Laughter bubbles from sidewalk cracks,
Echoes of kids playing tag, no lacks.
Dandelions dance in joyous spree,
While I trip over roots like a clumsy bee.

Each smile shared is a precious gem,
With passing cars playing a raucous hymn.
The postman winks, as he drops off the mail,
Life's little gifts, its own kind of trail.

So here's to the sunshine that warms the day,
To the quirky moments that come out to play.
In the light and laughter, we find our stride,
Sunlit sidewalks, our funny guide.

Lessons in Laundry Baskets

In the laundry basket, secrets dwell,
Matching socks that never gel.
Colors mix like a painter's spree,
I ponder life while sorting debris.

Tumble dryer spins tales in the heat,
Whispering gossip of each pair's feat.
A sock finds freedom while I despair,
As I chase down its mate without a care.

Detergent smiles with its bubbly pride,
Spinning tales as clothes take a ride.
Whites with colors become quite a mess,
Lessons in chaos—blessed distress!

So here in the wash, I chuckle and fold,
Each fabric story more precious than gold.
Finding joy in the spin and the tumble,
Life's simple truths in the laundry's shuffle.

Silence of a Sunday Afternoon

A napkin slides off the table with flair,
As I sip on tea, free from all care.
Sunday whispers with a lazy grin,
While dust motes dance, where do they begin?

My cat sprawls wide, a conqueror bold,
Claiming the couch, a throne of gold.
Ticking clocks sing a gentle tune,
As I ponder life by the light of noon.

The wind tickles trees, making them sway,
As the biscuits bake and send scents our way.
In the silence, laughter begins to bloom,
A ticklish tickle in the cozy room.

So I embrace the quiet, the still, the slow,
With crumbs in my lap and an idle glow.
In the calm of Sunday, we find our cheer,
With giggles and tea, life's treasures appear.

Heartbeats in the Familiar

A sock that lost its partner, oh!
Dancing on the floor alone,
The toaster pops, a morning show,
While coffee brews a love song tone.

The cat's conspiracy runs amok,
Chasing shadows like a pro,
The fridge hums like a rocking clock,
As leftovers threaten to overflow.

My slippers wear a sassy grin,
As if they know my every step,
The old couch creaks, lets me in,
Each laugh a secret that we kept.

Mismatched socks become my flair,
Each day a chuckle at the grind,
Life's quirks, oh great and rare,
In the mundane, joy we find.

Moments Wrapped in Ordinary

The milk's expired, oh what a thrill,
A yellow post-it rule my fate,
With every spill, a time to chill,
And laughter's just a fridge away.

A trip to town just to unwind,
Avoiding chaos like a pro,
The local cat is well-defined,
In every shop, it steals the show.

Random chats at the bus stop line,
A gossip tale or two to spare,
With every stop, a punchline divine,
Commuting's less dull with a flare.

The pizza box, the party's cape,
In crust we trust, the pineapples shine,
In every slice, a new escape,
Life's sweet laughter — oh so fine.

Relics of Daily Compassion

The neighbor's dog howls like a pro,
In sync with my morning strain,
Yet somehow, it's the best show,
In this circus we call plain.

A spilled drink at the dinner table,
A splash of chaos and surprise,
We laugh while trying to be stable,
Every crack brings joyous sighs.

The mailman waves, his hat askew,
Delivering tales, both new and old,
In every smile, a funny view,
Life unravels in stories bold.

Yet in the shambles of our day,
These moments make the shadows bright,
In simple things, we find the way,
With quirky hearts, we ignite.

The Intimacy of the Everyday

When laundry takes a daring flight,
The socks do tango in the breeze,
As watching them brings pure delight,
I giggle, daydreaming with ease.

The sunlight spills in like a jest,
The cereal, a crunchy ditty,
With every crunch, a tiny fest,
In this chaos, I find my city.

Each parking lot, a tiny play,
As carts collide, a clumsy race,
We shuffle through the odd ballet,
Strangers smile at the funny chase.

Oh, isn't life a juicy fruit?
With peels that hide the sweetest taste,
In everyday moments, we salute,
The humor life has laid to waste.

Lullabies of the Unremarkable

Socks on the floor, a dance of chance,
Coffee spills like everyday romance.
Dishes chatter in the sink's embrace,
Life is a circus, in a calm, wild space.

Toaster pops like it's had a grand show,
Pants mysteriously shrink, who could know?
The cat's grand performance, a leap and a flop,
In this sweet chaos, we laugh till we drop.

Unmade beds tell tales of dreams gone awry,
Where pillows are clouds and time drifts by.
Lost in the laundry, odd socks unite,
A vibrant parade of mismatched delight.

So let us sing tunes of the mundane,
In each silly moment, the joy is the gain.
From crumbs in the couch to the dust on the shelf,
Life's funny lullabies hum to oneself.

The Canvas of Daily Commuting

Rush hour stampede, a bizarre art show,
Where folks juggle phones, with a coffee to go.
Strangers exchange glances, a wink or a sigh,
In this daily gallery, we let out a cry.

Buses are canvases painted with smells,
Of breakfast burritos, and odd ringing bells.
The live soundtrack is laughter, a snore or a chat,
As someone debates if they like pine or sprat.

Each stop's a new story, a twist and a turn,
With quirky characters, the spotlight they earn.
And just as we place our dreams on the line,
The conductor announces, "You'll be just fine!"

So here's to the rides that shake us awake,
With moments of magic, each laugh is a cake.
In every commute, it's a moment to see,
The art of the average, our fun odyssey.

Ripples in the Stillness

A garden hose lies in the sun's warm grip,
Sprinkling laughter, with every little drip.
Ladybugs press plays on green leafy stages,
In this little cosmos, we laugh through the ages.

The old swing creaks like a wooden old man,
Telling jokes about life as best as it can.
Each gentle breeze whispers secrets it knows,
As we chase down the shadows where silliness grows.

There's wisdom in puddles where raindrops collide,
Where reflections of giggles are carefully tied.
Watch as the ants in their suits march along,
In the grand orchestra, they sing the sweet song.

So here in the stillness, we find all the jest,
In the ordinary, we're truly blessed.
With ripples of laughter, and joy's gentle stir,
Life's quiet moments, our hearts shall confer.

The Alphabet of the Unseen

In a world of whispers and giggles galore,
Letters dance like butterflies, who could ask for more?
A cat on the windowsill writes A, B, and C,
In a language so silly, just for you and me.

Fallen leaves paint stories, a rustling ballet,
As wind whispers secrets about yesterday.
Each rock has a riddle, each stick has a tale,
In this wild library, no detail is stale.

Laundry days feature characters that sing,
Folding up socks, they start a new fling.
Mismatched adventures where buttons confide,
In the quirky adventures, there's nothing to hide.

So laugh through the letters, embrace every scene,
In the grammar of giggles, the mundane is keen.
In the alphabet of all that we miss,
There's joy in the simple, pure pleasure and bliss.

Melodies in the Mundane

In the clatter of spoons and forks,
A symphony plays while the toaster quarks.
Dancing socks in the dryer's spin,
Each tumble whispers where joy begins.

Dust bunnies sway like they own the floor,
As vacuum hums out its roguish roar.
Coffee spills—a caffeinated art,
Laughter brews where the mad hatters start.

The fridge croaks like a grumpy old man,
Yet inside, treasures like leftovers span.
Jars of pickles, a sticky surprise,
In trivial moments, we find the prize.

Sunbeams invade through a window's glare,
Chasing shadows, they pirouette in air.
Each crack in the wall tells stories grand,
In tiny quirks, life takes a stand.

The Art of Domesticity

Mismatched socks on the laundry line,
Each pair a tale, each wrinkle a sign.
The dustpan grins, a silent friend,
In every chore, the giggles blend.

The kitchen timer sings off-key songs,
Pans clash like siblings, where chaos belongs.
A spatula dance with a saucepan lead,
In burnt toast moments, our hearts get fed.

Gardening gloves that are frayed and worn,
With weeds that laugh at the flowers born.
A rogue snail moves at a snail's pace,
As we chase laughter in life's warm embrace.

Through cluttered drawers, treasures abound,
Lost keys and marbles—oh, joy can be found!
In frames of dust and mismatched chairs,
We build our dreams in the little affairs.

Quiet Yesterdays

A forgotten sandwich hides in the fridge,
Nostalgia's feast beneath the age-old ridge.
The cat peeks out as memories swirl,
Of knitted scarves in a wobbly swirl.

Cochairs have tales only dust bunnies know,
As remote controls start to steal the show.
What sorcery lies in a coffee stain?
Quiet afternoons, we lose and gain.

The landline rings, a clumsy friend calls,
With wild stories of their afternoon brawls.
We sip herbal tea, let the laughter brew,
Chris missed the punchline—how can that be true?

Outside a kid roller-skates with flair,
While joyous chaos fills the sunlit air.
In every fumble, a nugget to keep,
Warm memories drift while we giggle and leap.

Serendipity in Small Talk

At the grocery store, a cart dance unfolds,
An avocado slips—I'm caught in the folds.
With a giggle, I shout, "Hey, catch that green!"
In everyday moments, joy's often seen.

Neighbors wave with cups of tea held high,
While gossip floats like balloons in the sky.
Each funny mishap, a tale spun with glee,
In laughter we find what it means to be free.

A cat meows like a diva in need,
As the mailman shares what's new on the feed.
With each friendly quirk, our smiles connect,
In the simplest exchanges, we find perfect wrecks.

The dog rolls over, a comedic delight,
As the sun dips low, painting skies bright.
In trivial chatter, a spark of the grand,
In laughter we knead, together we stand.

Chasing Shadows of Simplicity

In the morning light, I sip my tea,
A cat crosses my path, is it absurdity?
Life's little quirks, like spaghetti on toast,
Bring giggles and joy, they matter the most.

The mailman slips, a letter takes flight,
We laugh at the chaos, oh what a sight!
A dance with the dust as it floats in the air,
Simple things tickle, they light up despair.

A sock falls behind the old dusty chair,
Reminding me gently, of moments laid bare.
The twist of a joke, a pun that won't die,
In laughter, we find the sparks that imply.

So here's to the mornings, mundane and bright,
Chasing the shadows that dance with delight.
Life's little blunders, oh how they can shine,
In the ordinary, our hearts intertwine.

The Beauty in Lost Moments

In the fridge, I found a forgotten old pear,
A riddle of time that smells of despair.
Yet look at it closely, such beauty revealed,
It's a treasure of stories the fridge has concealed.

I tripped on a shoe and laughed at the sight,
Why do they hide, in the dark of the night?
Should I wear mismatched socks? What a delight!
In lost moments, life's flavor feels right.

My coffee spills out, like a wild little beast,
Creating a masterpiece, oh joy, at least!
A swirl of brown chaos on my white shirt,
Proof that perfection is often inert.

So I dance with the awkward, embrace every fall,
In the ordinary mishaps, I answer the call.
For beauty's not always in the grand, that's true,
But in finding the laughter that bubbles in you.

Echoes of the Commonplace

A spoon in my pocket, how did it get here?
Was it dreaming of soup, or just feeling sheer?
Ordinary objects whisper and cheer,
In the echoes of chaos, they disappear.

The neighbor's lawn gnome, it winks at the cat,
Confetti of gardens is where they're at!
Each clumsy moment, like slipping on ice,
Is a tale unfolding, oh isn't it nice?

The toaster's a wizard, it burns with such flair,
Turning bread to a masterpiece, crumbling care.
In crumbs lie the secrets of sad bread's retreat,
Each bite holds a laugh, a delicious defeat.

So let's toast to the mundane, the funny, the flat,
In echoes of laughter, that's where we're at.
The commonplace giggles, yes, they fill up the void,
In the silliness of life, we find joy unalloyed.

A Dance in the Dull

The clock ticks in rhythm, a dance so absurd,
Counting minutes as if they could be heard.
Yet in every tick-tock, a chuckle awaits,
In the jingle of tedium, joy insinuates.

The dust on the shelf starts to tango around,
As I join in the jig, feeling wonder abound.
A matinee show of the unwashed plates,
In happy reflections, life softly inflates.

The laundry that piles; a colorful mound,
Transforms into mountains where odd socks are found.
Every tumble and twist must have a soft score,
In the dull, there's a dance worth living for.

For life is a rhythm of mishaps and cheer,
Waltzing through moments, let go of the fear.
In laughter, the subtler notes play their part,
A dance in the dull, that's the beat of the heart.

Heartstrings of the Commonplace

In the coffee shop, I sip and stare,
A dog wears glasses, a sight quite rare.
The barista juggles foam and milk,
Like a circus act with charm and silk.

A man reads comics, laughs out loud,
While pigeons strut, feeling quite proud.
I giggle at life's simple trends,
As laughter swirls, the day transcends.

The clock ticks on, yet time stands still,
I ponder donuts, those sugary thrills.
In the chaos of crumbs and delight,
I find my purpose in every bite.

When life feels heavy, like a wet sock,
I lean on joy—my treasured rock.
In each silly moment, we find our groove,
Heartstrings dance, and our souls improve.

Sacred Seconds at Dusk

At dusk, the cicadas hum a tune,
As squirrels plot heists beneath the moon.
A neighbor's cat struts with a meow,
Like royalty here, beneath the bough.

The ice cream truck jingles down the street,
Kids chase after—oh, life is sweet!
A firefly blinks, I blink back too,
In simple moments, our hearts renew.

The clouds take shapes, a dragon, a shoe,
Imagination sparkles, it's nothing new.
I laugh at my thoughts as they swirl and spin,
In the dusk, that's where I truly begin.

As shadows stretch, I sip my tea,
Watching the world, just being me.
The sacred seconds, a playful jest,
Ordinary life truly is the best.

Marvels in the Mundanity

Perched upon the couch, I recline,
A crumb finds its way down the line.
The TV's full of shows so absurd,
As I search for snacks, my thoughts are stirred.

The laundry piles up, a mountain of woes,
Yet in every shirt, a story grows.
As I fold mismatched socks, there's a cheer,
Reminding me of a life I hold dear.

The goldfish swims in circles tight,
While I daydream of taking flight.
In the flicker of mundane, laughter brews,
Life's silly moments are the best of hues.

With coffee stains decorating my book,
I laugh at the chaos; I take a look.
In the mundane, there's magic spun,
A dance of the everyday, oh what fun!

Unringing the Bell of Complexity

In the kitchen chaos, pots collide,
While I attempt to bake and hide.
Flour on my nose, a cat on the shelf,
I giggle loudly, forgetting myself.

The phone won't stop, it buzzes away,
With notifications calling, "Come play!"
I scroll through memes, they crack me up,
Sometimes I wonder—did I fill my cup?

A spoon slips from grasp, plops in the stew,
Boiling over like my thoughts do.
Yet in wrapped-up moments, laughter finds space,
As I dance around with pie on my face.

The world's a circus, I join in the fun,
In the mess of it all, life's never done.
Unringing the bell, I embrace the jest,
In ordinary antics, I feel truly blessed.

Exploring the Depths of the Surface

In the cereal box, a treasure lies,
A prize for the brave, where Fortune flies.
I dive for a spoon, it's quite the quest,
To find little toys, who knew food's best?

Potholes in sidewalks, a dance and a trip,
Navigate wisely, don't lose your grip.
Cracks in the pavement, a story unfold,
What secrets they hide, legends untold!

A sock on the floor, it's a faithful mate,
Lost in the dryer, it meets its fate.
Yet in this odd world, with laughter and cheer,
Who knew laundry could spark such a leer?

Grapes in the fridge, a fruit medley treat,
Each pop is a burst, oh, life's little sweet.
In between chores, we find joy and glee,
In bubbles and bites, our hearts run free!

Timelessness in Textures

The feel of the carpet, a furry delight,
Underfoot, a cloud, can dance through the night.
With crumbs on the floor, it's a crunchy place,
A sprinkle of chaos, yet full of grace.

Each wrinkle of time on an old chair sat,
Tells tales of the family dog and the cat.
With coffee stains mottled like art on a wall,
Every sip savored feels like a ball.

The tick of the clock, with rhythms so grand,
Is it spring yet, or winter hand-in-hand?
Yet through all the ticking, a chuckle we greet,
In moments of stillness, life's glitchy beat.

Old jeans with patches, a vintage affair,
Belly laughs echo from memories rare.
In scrapes and in freckles, it's joy that's penned,
In textures of laughter, the ordinary blends!

Ordinary Paths to Infinite Journeys

Strolling down streets with a latte in hand,
The splashes of colors, oh, life's merry band.
A squirrel on a quest, stealing fries with a grin,
In moments like these, where adventure begins.

An elevator ride, a shared awkward glance,
The pause of the lift, a made-up romance.
As we both exit at floors twenty-three,
What stories have we? Just wait and see.

In park benches worn down by time's gentle hands,
We sit with our musings, as laughter expands.
A fleeting moment, a shared breath of air,
The magic is felt, like wisps in our hair.

In grocery lines, life can be sheer bliss,
With coupons in hand, oh, don't you dare miss.
In the ordinary, chaos paints vibrant hues,
With laughter and quirks, we've nothing to lose!

Flickering Lights of Recognition

The fridge hums a tune, a symphony so bright,
Late-night snacks calling, oh, what a delight!
Mismatched Tupperware sings out a chorus,
Finding old leftovers, health risks before us!

The cat on the window, sun-soaked and keen,
Judging my life like a royal unseen.
With a flick of a tail, and a yawn not so shy,
Who knew a furball could reach for the sky?

Socks that don't match, oh where did they go?
In the depths of the laundry, I'm putting on a show.
Each odd little sock sings a tale of its own,
Our mismatched adventures have finally grown.

Buzzing lightbulbs flicker, a disco of dreams,
In the flickering glow, the absurd truly beams.
In the dance with the mundane, joy manifests,
Amidst all the chaos, it's laughter that rests!

Forgotten Corners of the World

In shadows where the dust bunnies play,
A sock with a hole dreams of a grand ballet.
Old coffee mugs dance a quiet tune,
While mismatched spoons argue over the moon.

A cat in a box claims it's a throne,
The clock hands get lazy, they've all overgrown.
Chairs creak with tales of when they were young,
As crumbs from the past hum the songs once sung.

Beneath the couch, treasures lie in wait,
A jellybean army meets a toy alligator's fate.
Dust gathers tales as it floats through the light,
In forgotten corners, the ordinary takes flight.

The Richness of Repetition

The toaster pops toast, it's breakfast time,
While I ponder the wonders of crunchy rhyme.
Cereal swirls in the milk like it's ballet,
Each spoonful a ritual, come what may.

The kettle whistles, a shrill morning song,
As routines march forward, each day feels long.
Socks in the dryer perform their wild dance,
A spin cycle of chaos, oh what a chance!

The neighbors' dog barks like he's got some news,
While I sip my coffee, crafting quirky views.
The beauty of boredom, oh what a thrill,
In this cycle of life, we trip but we'll spill.

Hues of Routine

Sunlight drips through the kitchen door,
While I contemplate what yesterday wore.
Every mug has a smirk, a wink or a pout,
As I brew another plan that's bound to flout.

The broom plays the scepter in my daily parade,
Sweeping up hopes that have slightly decayed.
The fridge hums a tune of pickles and cheese,
As the clock strikes the hour, I'm on my knees.

Laundry leaps from the basket to fight,
Socks forming alliances in the fading light.
Each button I sew tells the tale of a tear,
Just hues of routine, pulled from thin air.

Speak Softly, Life Will Listen

The old chair creaks as wisdom takes a seat,
While the cat stares intensely, oh so discreet.
Pickles hold secrets in their glassy dome,
And the dust on the shelf keeps stories at home.

Through mundane chatter, profound thoughts arise,
As I walk past the garden, where a worm ties its ties.
With every small miracle, giggles take flight,
In the quiet of chaos, we find our delight.

The teapot whistles a soft like sigh,
While the sugar bowl dreams, and the creamer flies high.
So speak softly, my friend, it's wise to persist,
For life is a riddle with moments of bliss.

The Art of Watching Clouds

A fluffy sheep drifts by with grace,
I wonder if it dreams of a race.
The sky's a canvas, blue and wide,
Where time gets lost and worries hide.

Puffy popcorn, a whale's huge tail,
A giant sandwich, or a ship to sail.
With every shift, the stories erupt,
Nature's comedy, just wait and sup!

What a talent to sit and behold,
As fluffy dreams in the sky unfold.
From daydreaming, I cannot escape,
The wonders above in every shape.

Grace Found in the Grit

I spill my coffee, it splashes around,
In this clumsy ballet, grace can be found.
The floor's a canvas, life's art is pure,
With each slip up, I find my allure.

A stubborn piece of lint, what a foe,
Sticking to my pants like it's putting on a show.
I try to brush it off, but it fights back,
Laughing at my efforts, an attack!

While dishes pile high, the sink's a scene,
A soap bubble party, both messy and clean.
In every soggy moment, I find a cheer,
Who knew grits and giggles could bring good cheer?

A Sequence of Simple Surprises

The toast pops up, a sudden start,
Landing with a clatter, not so smart.
Jam rolls off like a slippery spy,
Sticky missions where toast can fly!

I trip on my shoelace, oh dear me,
The carpet's a monster, it's quite a spree!
Yet laughter bubbles up, oh what a day,
In these tiny mishaps, I find my way.

A cat leaps out from behind the couch,
With a startled jump, my heart does slouch.
Chasing flies with a dash and a swat,
In their wild dance, all worries forgot!

Socks on a Clothesline

Two socks sway in the breeze so bright,
A pair so mismatched, but still a sight.
They dance with joy, they twirlingly glide,
In the sun's warm embrace, their pride can't hide.

One's spotted, the other's stripes galore,
A fashion statement, who needs more?
In this carefree moment, they seem to sing,
Ballet of laundry, joy's the real king!

They whisper tales of adventures so grand,
From muddy puddles to golden sand.
From the mundane, their stories derive,
Socks on a line, oh, how they thrive!

www.ingramcontent.com/pod-product-compliance
Lightning Source LLC
Chambersburg PA
CBHW051659160426
43209CB00004B/951